from My Bondage and My Freedom

by Frederick Douglas

LOOKING FORWARD

In this excerpt from his autobiography, Frederick Douglass tells of his quest for education and his undying desire for freedom.

© 2002 by Perfection Learning®
Please visit our website at:
www.perfectionlearning.com

When ordering this book, please specify:
ISBN 978-0-7891-5663-1 or 79218

eBook: ISBN 978-1-5311-2638-4 or 79218D

9 10 11 12 13   PP   25 24 23 22 21

Printed in the United States of America

WORDS TO WATCH FOR

Here are some words that may be unfamiliar. Use this list as a guide to better understanding. Examine it before you begin to read.

atone—make up; remedy
benevolence—kindness; compassion
censure—criticize; judge
chafed—troubled; tormented
compliance—obedience; cooperation
divest—rid; relieve
expedients—tools; means
prudence—common sense; caution; wisdom
redolent—suggestive; remindful
unseared—not hardened by experience; uncalloused

from My Bondage and My Freedom

by Frederick Douglass

I lived in the family of Master Hugh, at Baltimore, seven years, during which time—as the almanac makers say of the weather—my condition was variable. The most interesting feature of my history here, was my learning to read and write, under somewhat marked disadvantages. In attaining this knowledge, I was compelled to resort to indirections by no means congenial to my nature, and which were really humiliating to me. My mistress—who had begun to teach me—was suddenly checked in her benevolent design, by the strong advice of her husband. In faithful compliance with this advice, the good lady had not only ceased to instruct me, herself, but had set her face as a flint against my learning to read by any means. It is due, however, to my mistress to say, that she did not adopt this course in all its stringency at the first. She either thought it unnecessary, or she lacked the depravity indispensable to shutting me up in mental darkness. It was, at least, necessary for her to have some training, and some hardening, in the exercise of the slaveholder's prerogative, to make her equal to forgetting my human nature and character, and to treating me as a

4

thing destitute of a moral or an intellectual nature. Mrs. Auld—my mistress—was, as I have said, a most kind and tenderhearted woman; and, in the humanity of her heart, and the simplicity of her mind, she set out, when I first went to live with her, to treat me as she supposed one human being ought to treat another.

It is easy to see, that, in entering upon the duties of a slaveholder, some little experience is needed. Nature has done almost nothing to prepare men and women to be either slaves or slaveholders. Nothing but rigid training, long persisted in, can perfect the character of the one or the other. One cannot easily forget to love freedom; and it is as hard to cease to respect that natural love in our fellow creatures. On entering upon the career of a slaveholding mistress, Mrs. Auld was singularly deficient; nature, which fits nobody for such an office, had done less for her than any lady I had known. It was no easy matter to induce her to think and to feel that the curly-headed boy, who stood by her side, and even leaned on her lap; who was loved by little Tommy, and who loved little Tommy in turn; sustained to her only the relation of a chattel. I was *more* than that, and she felt me to be more than that. I could talk and sing; I could laugh and weep; I could reason and remember; I could love and hate. I was human, and she, dear lady, knew and felt me to be so. How could

5

she, then, treat me as a brute, without a mighty struggle with all the noble powers of her own soul. That struggle came, and the will and power of the husband was victorious. Her noble soul was overthrown; but, he that overthrew it did not, himself, escape the consequences. He, not less than the other parties, was injured in his domestic peace by the fall.

When I went into their family, it was the abode of happiness and contentment. The mistress of the house was a model of affection and tenderness. Her fervent piety and watchful uprightness made it impossible to see her without thinking and feeling—"that woman is a Christian." There was no sorrow nor suffering for which she had not a tear, and there was no innocent joy for which she did not a smile. She had bread for the hungry, clothes for the naked, and comfort for every mourner that came within her reach. Slavery soon proved its ability to divest her of these excellent qualities, and her home of its early happiness. Conscience cannot stand much violence. Once thoroughly broken down, *who* is he that can repair the damage? It may be broken toward the slave, on Sunday, and toward the master on Monday. It cannot endure such shocks. It must stand entire, or it does not stand at all. If my condition waxed bad, that of the family waxed not better. The first step, in the wrong direction, was the violence done to nature and to conscience, in arresting the benevolence that would have enlightened my young mind. In ceasing to instruct me, she must begin to justify herself *to* herself; and, once consenting to take sides in such a debate, she was riveted to her position. One needs very little knowledge of moral philosophy, to see *where* my mistress now landed. She finally became even more violent in her opposition to my learning to read, than was her husband himself. She was not satisfied with simply doing as well as her husband had commanded her, but seemed resolved to better his instruction. Nothing appeared to make my poor mistress—after her turning toward the downward path—more angry, than seeing me, seated in some nook or corner, quietly reading a book or a newspaper. I have had her rush at me, with the utmost fury, and snatch from my hand such newspaper or book, with something of the wrath and consternation which a traitor might be supposed to feel on being discovered in a plot by some dangerous spy.

Mrs. Auld was an apt woman, and the advice of her husband, and her own experience, soon demonstrated, to her entire satisfaction, that education and slavery are incompatible with each other. When this conviction was thoroughly established, I was most narrowly watched in all my movements. If I remained in a separate room from the family for any considerable length of time, I was sure to be suspected of having a book, and was at once called upon to give an account of myself. All this, however, was entirely *too late*. The first, and never to be retraced step had been taken. In teaching me the alphabet, in the days of her simplicity and kindness, my mistress had given me the "inch," and now, no ordinary precaution could prevent me from taking the "ell."[1]

Seized with a determination to learn to read, at any cost, I hit upon many expedients to accomplish the desired end. The plea which I mainly adopted, and the one by which I was most successful, was that of using my young white playmates, with whom I met in the street, as teachers. I used to carry, almost constantly, a copy of Webster's spelling book in my pocket; and, when sent on errands, or when play time was allowed me, I would step, with my young friends, aside, and take a lesson in spelling. I generally paid my tuition fee to the boys, with bread, which I also carried in my pocket. For a single biscuit, any of my hungry little comrades would give me a lesson more valuable to me than bread. Not everyone, however, demanded this consideration, for there were those who took

---

[1] *ell*: a measure of length equal to forty-five inches.

pleasure in teaching me, whenever I had the chance to be taught by them. I am strongly tempted to give the names of two or three of those little boys, as a slight testimonial of the gratitude and affection I bear them, but prudence forbids; not that it would injure me, but it might, possibly, embarrass them; for it is almost an unpardonable offense to do anything, directly or indirectly, to promote a slave's freedom, in a slave state. It is enough to say, of my warm-hearted little play fellows, that they lived on Philpot Street, very near Durgin & Bailey's shipyard.

Although slavery was a delicate subject, and very cautiously talked about among grown-up people in Maryland, I frequently talked about it— and that very freely—with the white boys. I would, sometimes, say to them, while seated on a curbstone or a cellar door, "I wish I could be free, as you will be when you get to be men." "You will be free, you know, as soon as you are twenty-one, and can go where you like, but I am a slave for life. Have I not as good a right to be free as you have?" Words like these, I observed, always troubled them; and I had no small satisfaction in wringing from the boys, occasionally, that fresh and bitter condemnation of slavery, that springs from nature, unseared and unperverted. Of all conscience let me have those to deal with which have not been bewildered by the cares of life. I do not remember ever to have met with a *boy*, while I was in slavery, who defended the slave system; but I have often had boys to console me, with the hope that something would yet occur, but which I might be made free. Over and over again, they have told me, that "they believed *I* had as good a right to be free as *they* had"; and that "they did not believe God ever made anyone to be a slave." The reader will easily see, that such little conversations with my play fellows, had no tendency to weaken my love of liberty, nor to render me contented with my condition as a slave.

When I was about thirteen years old, and had succeeded in learning to read, every increase of knowledge, especially respecting the free states, added something to the almost intolerable burden of the thought—"I am a slave for life." To my bondage I saw no end. It was a terrible reality, and I shall never be able to tell how sadly that thought chafed my young spirit. Fortunately, or unfortunately, about this time in my life, I had made enough money to buy what was then a very popular schoolbook, the *Columbian Orator*. I bought this addition to my library, of Mr. Knight, on Thames Street, Fell's Point, Baltimore, and paid him fifty cents for it. I was first led to buy this book, by hearing some little boys say they were going to learn some little pieces out of it for the Exhibition. This volume was, indeed, a rich treasure, and every opportunity afforded me, for a time, was spent in diligently perusing it. . . . The dialogue and the speeches were all redolent of the principles of liberty, and poured floods of light on the nature and character of slavery. As I read, behold! the very discontent so graphically predicted by Master Hugh, had already come upon me. I was no longer the light-hearted, gleesome boy, full of mirth and play, as when I landed first at Baltimore. Knowledge had come. . . . The knowledge opened my eyes to the horrible pit, and revealed the teeth of the frightful dragon that was ready to pounce upon me, but it opened no way for my escape. I have often wished myself a beast, or a bird—anything, rather than a slave. I was wretched and gloomy, beyond my ability to describe. I was too thoughtful to be happy. It was this everlasting thinking which distressed and tormented me; and yet there was no getting rid of the subject of my thoughts. All nature was redolent of it. Once awakened by the silver trump of knowledge, my spirit was roused to eternal wakefulness. Liberty! the inestimable birthright of every man, had, for me, converted every object into an asserter of this great right. It was heard in every sound, and beheld in every object. It was ever present, to torment me with a sense of my wretched condition. The more beautiful and charming were the smiles of nature, the more horrible and desolate was my condition. I saw nothing without seeing it, and I heard nothing without hearing it. I do not exaggerate, when I say, that it looked from every star, smiled in every calm, breathed in every wind, and moved in every storm.

I have no doubt that my state of mind had something to do with the change in the treatment adopted, by my once kind mistress toward me. I can easily believe, that my leaden, downcast, and discontented look, was very offensive to her. Poor lady! She did not know my trouble, and I dared not tell her. Could I have freely made her acquainted with the real state of my mind, and given her the reasons therefor, it might have been well for both of us. Her abuse of me fell upon me like the blows of the false prophet upon his ass; she did not know that an *angel* stood in the way; and—such is the relation of master and slave—I could not tell her. Nature had made us *friends*; slavery made us *enemies*. My interests were in a direction opposite to hers, and we both had our private thoughts and plans. She aimed to keep me ignorant and I resolved to know, although knowledge only increased my discontent. My feelings were not the result of any marked cruelty in the treatment I received; they sprung from the consideration of my being a slave at all. It was *slavery*—not its mere *incidents*—that I hated. I had been cheated. I saw through the attempt to keep me in ignorance. . . . The feeding and clothing me well, could not atone for taking my liberty from me. The smiles of my mistress could not remove the deep sorrow that dwelt in my young bosom. Indeed, these, in time, came only to deepen my sorrow. She had changed; and the reader will see that I had changed, too. We were both victims to the same overshadowing evil—*she*, as mistress, *I*, as slave. I will not censure her harshly; she cannot censure me, for she knows I speak but the truth, and have acted in my opposition to slavery, just as she herself would have acted, in a reverse of circumstances.

Frederick Douglass

Frederick Douglass was born in Maryland around 1818, but since records were not kept of the birth of slaves, he was never sure of his exact age. Douglass was named Frederick Augustus Washington Bailey after his mother Harriet Bailey, a field hand on a plantation 12 miles from where he was raised. Douglass was probably the son of his white slave master, Aaron Anthony.

In 1825, Douglass was sent to Baltimore to serve as a houseboy for Hugh and Sophia Auld, relatives of Anthony. Because there were no schools for slaves, Douglass received no formal education as a child, but he did learn to read with the help of Mrs. Auld. By the time Hugh Auld put a stop to his wife's teachings, Douglass had learned enough to carry on by himself.

When Hugh Auld died a few years later, Douglass passed into the possession of Thomas Auld, Anthony's son-in-law. Douglass infuriated the younger Auld by refusing to address him as "master." Determined to crush the spirit of the young slave, Auld hired Douglass out to Edward Covey, a "slave breaker." Covey worked and whipped the sixteen-year-old unmercifully, but after six months Douglass struck back and attacked Covey in a barn. His triumph over the white man later caused Douglass to write, "This battle with Mr. Covey was the turning point in my career as a slave. . . . My long-crushed spirit rose, cowardice departed, bold defiance took its place; and I now resolved that, however long I might remain a slave in form, the day had passed forever when I could be a slave in fact."

In 1838, dressed in a sailor's uniform and carrying false identification papers provided by a free black seaman, Douglas escaped slavery and managed to reach New York City. He married and took the name of Douglass from the hero of a romantic novel, *Lady of the Lake*, by Sir Walter Scott. Soon after, the newly married couple moved to New Bedford, Massachusetts, where Douglass began attending antislavery meetings. After being called upon at one of these meetings to speak, he was urged to become an antislavery lecturer. His speeches were so eloquent, however, that the public soon began to wonder if he had ever indeed been a slave. To remove this doubt, Douglass published his autobiography *The Narrative of the Life of Frederick Douglass, an American Slave* in 1845. That same year he went to England, largely because of the danger he still faced as a fugitive slave, especially after the release of his book.

Douglass carried the antislavery movement to England and became officially free when his British friends paid $700 to purchase his freedom from his former master. Two years later, he returned to America and began publishing the *North Star*, a newspaper devoted to the abolition of slavery. In 1855, he published a revised version of his life's story, titled *My Bondage and My Freedom*, which did much to further his cause.

When the Civil War began, Douglass worked with the Underground Railroad, the secret network of abolitionists who helped people held in slavery escape to freedom. He also helped recruit African American soldiers for the Union army. Two of his sons served in the 54th Massachusetts Regiment, made up entirely of African American volunteers.

Eventually Douglass moved to Washington, D.C., where he held various national service positions, including U.S. Marshal for the District of Columbia, and diplomatic positions in Haiti and the Dominican Republic. He died in 1895 but is remembered today as a courageous defender of human rights. "To those who have suffered in slavery I can say I, too, have suffered," Douglass once said. "To those who have battled for liberty, brotherhood and citizenship I can say I, too, have battled."

I. THE STORY LINE
A. Digging for Facts

1. Mrs. Auld, Frederick's mistress, taught young Douglass (a) to cook; (b) to read; (c) the ways of gentlemen.

2. According to Douglass, Mrs. Auld was (a) a kind and tenderhearted woman; (b) cruel to her slaves; (c) "master" of her house.

3. Once Mr. Auld "advised" his wife to stop teaching Frederick, Mrs. Auld (a) continued to teach the boy behind her husband's back; (b) allowed her son Tommy to take over Frederick's instruction; (c) became cold and angry toward Frederick.

4. According to Douglass, nature has prepared people to be (a) masters but not slaves; (b) neither masters nor slaves; (c) slaves but not masters.

5. Once Mrs. Auld stopped teaching Douglass, he (a) lost all interest in learning; (b) hired a tutor; (c) continued on his own.

6. Douglass does not give the names of his white playmates because doing so might (a) cause them to hate him; (b) embarrass them; (c) get him into serious trouble.

7. According to Douglass, in Maryland, slavery was a (a) delicate subject; (b) much talked-about subject; (c) strictly forbidden subject.

8. When Douglass talks to his white playmates about the system of slavery, the boys often (a) defend the system; (b) refuse to talk about the system; (c) condemn the system.

9. Knowledge, according to Douglass, caused (a) his life to be more tolerable and even happy at times; (b) him to understand the slavery system better; (c) him to become unhappy in his plight as a slave.

10. In respect to his relationship with Mrs. Auld, Douglass says (a) nature made them enemies; slavery made them friends; (b) nature made them friends; slavery made them enemies; (c) nature made them enemies; slavery reinforced the hatred between them.

B. Probing for Theme

A *theme* is a central message of a piece of literature. Read the thematic statements below. Which one best applies to this excerpt from *My Bondage and My Freedom*? Be prepared to support your opinion.

1. Certain circumstances can cause drastic personality changes in people.

2. Slavery and education do not mix.

3. The system of slavery is hard on both slaves and masters.

II. IN SEARCH OF MEANING

1. What was Mrs. Auld like when Douglass first met her? What kind of person did she become?

2. What does Douglass mean when he uses the metaphor "shutting me up in mental darkness"?

3. Why did Mrs. Auld stop teaching Douglass how to read? Why, do you think, did she undergo such a drastic change of attitude toward him at that point?

4. Explain Douglass's statement: "Nature has done almost nothing to prepare men and women to be either slaves or slaveholders."

5. According to Douglass, why was it particularly hard on Mrs. Auld to be a mistress to slaves?

6. What happened to the Auld home as a result of Mrs. Auld's change?

7. How does Douglass manage to continue his education once Mrs. Auld stops teaching him?

8. When Douglass questions his white playmates about the slavery system, more often than not they respond by echoing his sentiments—that he has a right to be free. How does this affect young Douglass?

9. What was Douglass like when he arrived in Baltimore as a little boy? How did education change him?

10. Explain Douglass's statement about his relationship with Mrs. Auld: "Nature had made us *friends*; slavery made us *enemies*."

III. DEVELOPING WORD POWER

Exercise A

Each of the following words appears in a sentence taken directly from the excerpt. Read the sentence, and then select the correct meaning from the four choices.

1. compliance

   "In faithful *compliance* with this advice, the good lady had not only ceased to instruct me, herself, but had set her face as a flint against my learning to read by any means."

   a. resentment   c. obedience

   b. compromise   d. violation

2. divest

   "Slavery soon proved its ability to *divest* her of these excellent qualities, and her home of it its early happiness."

   a. grant   c. annoy

   b. alert   d. rid

3. benevolence

"The first step, in the wrong direction, was the violence done to nature and to conscience, in arresting the *benevolence* that would have enlightened my young mind."

a. kindness   c. attempt

b. intelligence   d. force

4. expedients

"Seized with a determination to learn to read, at any cost, I hit upon many *expedients* to accomplish the desired end."

a. accidents   c. circumstances

b. means   d. fortunes

5. prudence

"I am strongly tempted to give the names of two or three of those little boys, as a slight testimonial of the gratitude and affection I bear them, but *prudence* forbids . . ."

a. fear   c. hesitation

b. caution   d. embarrassment

6. unseared

". . . and I had no small satisfaction in wringing from the boys, occasionally, that fresh and bitter condemnation of slavery, that springs from nature, *unseared* and unperverted."

a. not critical   c. not guilty

b. not aware   d. not hardened

7. chafed

"It was a terrible reality, and I shall never be able to tell how sadly that thought *chafed* my young spirit."

a. scolded   c. stunted

b. tormented   d. affected

8. redolent

"The dialogue and the speeches were all *redolent* of the principles of liberty, and poured floods of light on the nature and character of slavery."

a. empty   c. suggestive

b. full   d. fearful

9. atone

"The feeding and clothing me well, could not *atone* for taking my liberty from me."

a. make up   c. be blamed

b. count   d. give a reason

10. censure

"I will not *censure* [Mrs. Auld] harshly . . ."

a. treat   c. judge

b. talk to   d. observe

Exercise B

Below is a list of vocabulary words (or a form of each) from the story. Choose the word that best completes the sentences that follow the list.

a. atone   f. divest

b. benevolence   g. expedient

c. censure   h. prudence

d. chafed   i. redolent

e. compliance   j. unseared

1. "Investing in that shaky business will surely __?__ you of your savings," the financial adviser told her client.

2. The restaurant was popular with the older crowd because it was __?__ of the 1950s .

3. At the suggestion that inmates be given television sets, the senator replied, "Prisons are not supposed to be entertaining. Prisons are places where people __?__ for their crimes. "

4. In __?__ with the new law, the company installed drinking fountains on every floor.

5. "We must find another __?__ to achieve our goals, now that our funding has been cut off," Mrs. Alvarez told her staff.

6. The elderly woman treated the neighborhood children with __?__, allowing them to play in her yard and bringing them lemonade and cookies.

7. "You acted with __?__ when you decided not to go to the unchaperoned party, and we're proud of you," Mr. Chen told his daughter.

8. __?__ by life, the children treated one another equally and kindly.

9. "I refuse to __?__ Mayor Tinsley," Mr. Erickson said his neighbors. "At least he tried to accomplish something, even if he failed."

10. The injustice of being accused of something her sister did __?__ Marina.

IV. IMPROVING WRITING SKILLS

Exercise A

Choose one of the following activities.

1. A *character sketch* is a short piece of writing that describes a person's physical appearance and personality. While this selection does not reveal what Douglass looked like, it certainly reveals a lot about his personality. Write a character sketch of Frederick Douglass based on the information in this selection.

2. Write the dialogue Master Hugh and his wife might have had about teaching Douglass to read. Keep in mind that Mrs. Auld was more than likely against her husband's "advice" at the beginning of the conversation.

Exercise B

The philosopher Epictetus once said, "Only the educated are free." What does this statement mean? Based on what you now know about Frederick Douglass, how do you think he would have responded to it? Explain your thoughts in a well-developed paragraph.

V. THINGS TO WRITE OR TALK ABOUT

1. In your opinion, is it possible for people to undergo such a complete personality change as Mrs. Auld did? Why or why not?

2. Douglass says that nature does not prepare anyone to be a slave or a master. What is hard about being a slave? about being a master? Which would be harder for you?

3. Why do you think Douglass's white playmates treated him as they did? Do you think that by the time they reached adulthood they approved of the system of slavery? Why or why not?

4. How can you tell by this selection that Douglass was a very intelligent man? What other characteristics of Douglass's does this selection reveal?

5. If Douglass were alive today, how do you think he would feel about the situation of African Americans?

ANSWER KEY

I. THE STORY LINE
A. Digging for Facts

1.	b	6.	b
2.	a	7.	a
3.	c	8.	c
4.	b	9.	c
5.	c	10.	b

B. Probing for Theme

Students may elect to support any of the three choices. The suggested answer is *Slavery and education do not mix.* When Douglass arrived in Baltimore, he was a "light-hearted, gleesome boy, full of mirth and play," and as long as Douglass did not have the means to compare his situation with that of free people, he remained that way. Once Mrs. Auld began to teach him to read, however, he became aware of the opportunities he would never be offered as a nonfree man. "The knowledge opened my eyes to the horrible pit, and revealed the teeth of the frightful dragon that was ready to pounce on me," he says. "It was ever present, to torment me with a sense of my wretched condition." Education, then, made him aware of his situation and resentful of being a slave, and a resentful slave does not make a good slave.

III. DEVELOPING WORD POWER

Exercise A

1. compliance

    c. obedience

2. divest

    d. rid

3. benevolence

    a. kindness

4. expedients

    b. means

5. prudence

    b. caution

6. unseared

    d. not hardened

7. chafed

    b. tormented

8. redolent

    c. suggestive

9. atone

    a. make up

10. censure

    c. judge

Exercise B

1.	(f)	divest
2.	(i)	redolent
3.	(a)	atone
4.	(e)	compliance
5.	(g)	expedient
6.	(b)	benevolence
7.	(h)	prudence
8.	(j)	unseared
9.	(c)	censure
10.	(d)	chafed